# The Ultimate Micro Fliers

# TOP THAT! Kids™

Published by Top That! Publishing Inc.
25031 W. Avenue Stanford, Suite #60, Valencia, CA 91355
www.topthatpublishing.com
Top That! Kids is trademark of Top That! Publishing Inc.
Copyright © 2005 Top That! Publishing plc

# Let's Fly

**This is your chance to become an ace at stunts and glides as you make models of some of the world's greatest flying machines.**

## Making the Micro Fliers

**1.** Gather all the pieces for your chosen model. Each model fits together easily and there's no need for special tools or materials.

**2.** Hold the body of the model and push the wing through the central slot. Make sure the "F" marked on the wing faces forward. If the model has more than one set of wings, remember to slot them onto the aircraft's body.

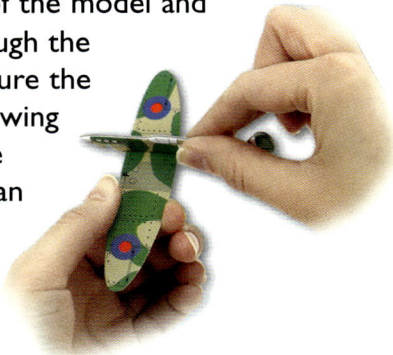

**3.** Now slide the tail in place. Push it through the slot on the back of the body.

**4.** Place a small piece of sticky putty on the nose to add the correct weight and balance.

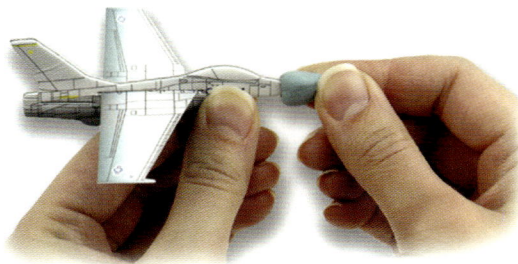

The rockets are made in much the same way as the planes. Gently push the solid rocket part through the central slot of the matching piece. Then, push it backward so that the groove at the tail end holds it in place.

**Tip:** Be careful not to bend any parts as this could affect the flight.

# Take Off

**There are two types of micro flier in this kit. Each type will need to be launched differently.**

## Power Launch

Some micro fliers have a notch underneath. These need to be launched using the catapult provided in the kit. To prepare the catapult, feed the rubber band into the grooves at the end, then hook it around the plastic pin in the center. Hook the rubber band onto the notch in the micro flier body. Pull the flier back and release it to launch!

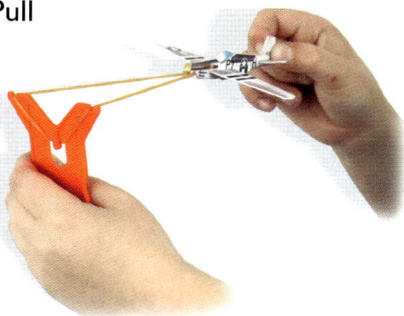

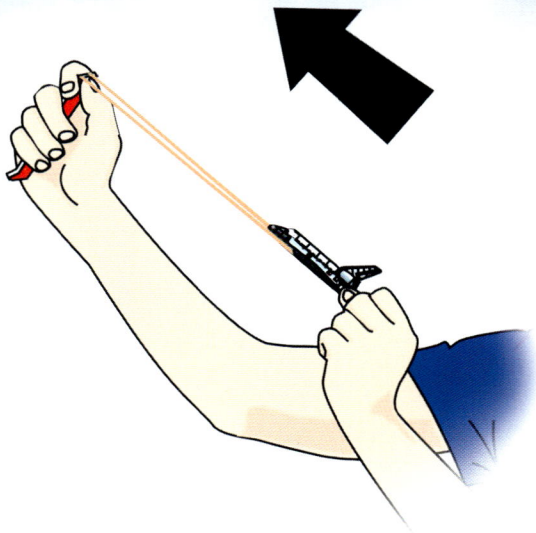

## Manual Take Off

The secret to manual take off is in the throw. Using your thumb and forefinger, hold the micro flier just behind the nose, then throw it gently into the air.

## Safety Warning

Here is a list of rules which every good pilot should follow:
- always launch your micro fliers in an open space away from roads and cars. Make sure you have plenty of room to run without getting run over;
- NEVER launch your micro fliers at anyone or anything;
- do not lean over your micro flier while you are trying to launch it; and
- know when to abort the mission. If you can't reach your micro flier safely, leave it—you have plenty of others to play with.

# V2 rocket

**The V2 rocket was built by a German research team led by a man called Werner von Braun in 1937.**

The V2 rocket was the world's first long-range ballistic missile. It was one of the most devastating weapons used by the Germans at the end of World War II.

In 1946 Werner von Braun surrendered his services to America to help develop the U.S. space program.

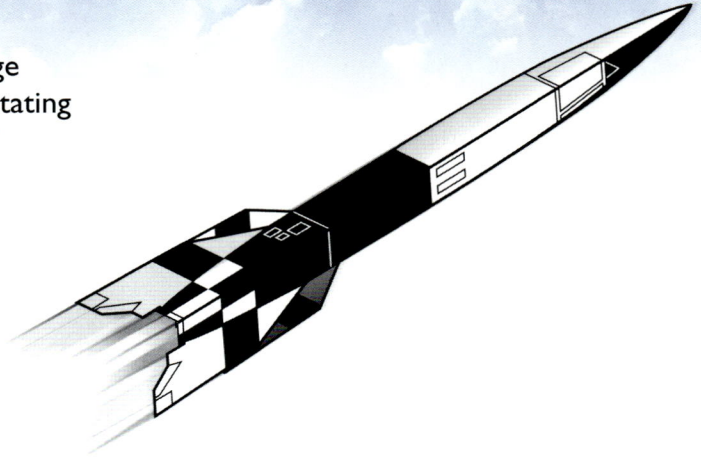

# Vostok

**On April 12, 1961, the Russian Vostok A1 rocket carried the first human into space; his name was Yuri Gagarin. The mission lasted for 108 minutes.**

Later Vostok missions included the involvement of the world's first woman cosmonaut, Valentina Tereshkova.

A crater on the far side of the Moon is named after Yuri Gagarin.

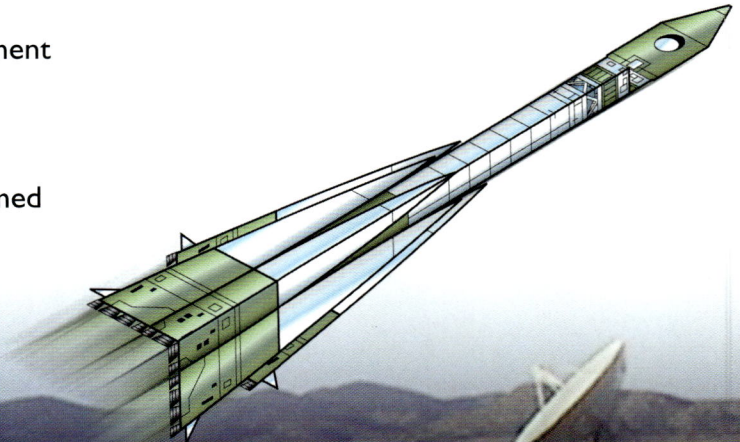

# Mercury Redstone

**On May 5, 1961, the Mercury Redstone rocket was launched from the Cape Canaveral launch site.**

It powered the United States' first astronaut into space; his name was Alan Bartlett Shepard.

The Mercury Redstone rocket is capable of 78,000 pounds of thrust at launch.

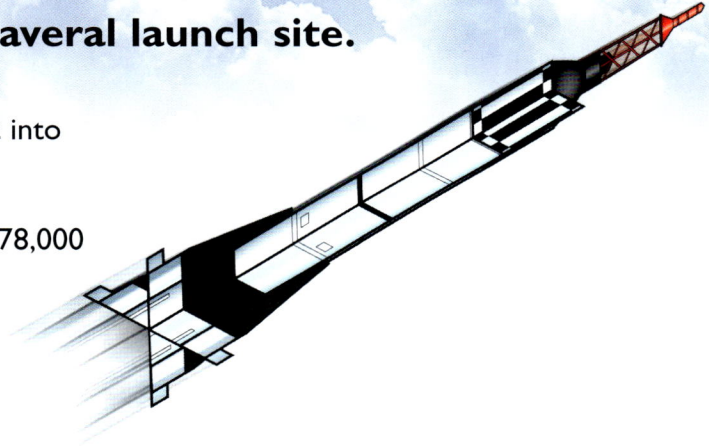

# Mercury Atlas

**This Mercury Atlas rocket carried John Glenn's spacecraft into Earth's orbit, making him the first American to ever orbit Earth.**

It was originally designed as an intercontinental ballistic missile (ICBM).

Atlas has three engines and two boosters to help it reach orbital velocity.

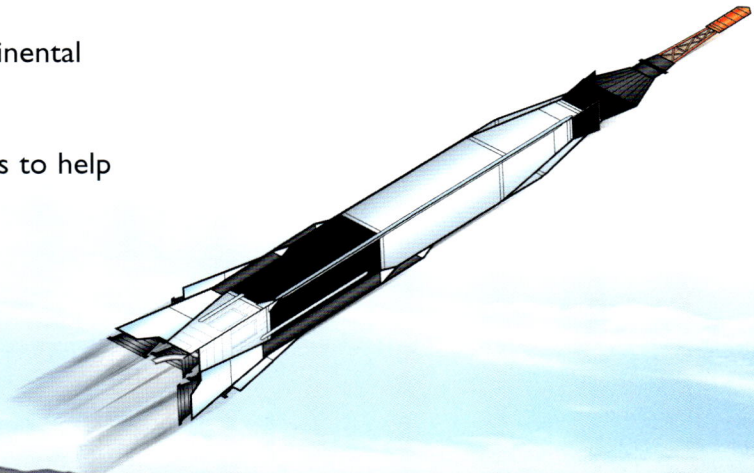

# Saturn V

On July 16, 1969, a Saturn V rocket powered U.S.A.'s Apollo 11 spacecraft to the Moon. Four days later Neil Armstrong and Edwin "Buzz" Aldrin walked on the Moon.

Saturn V rockets have been used for thirteen space missions, including ten manned missions.

The Saturn V rocket is as tall as a 33-storey building.

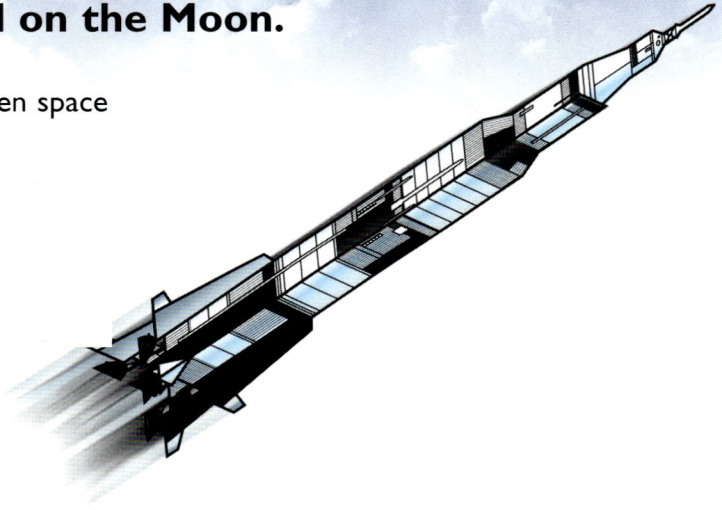

# Ariane 5

European Ariane rockets are commercial space carriers which can be hired by any country that wants to place a satellite in orbit above Earth.

There are six versions of the Ariane rocket, and all of them are completely computer controlled.

The Ariane rockets are launched from a massive launch site in French Guiana, South America.

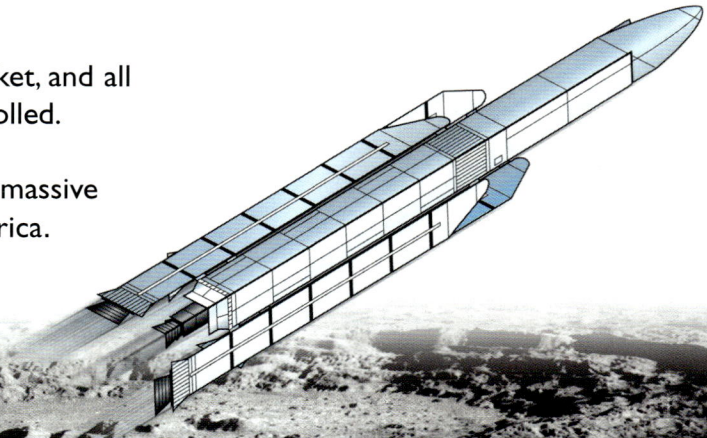

# Columbia

**The first space shuttle, *Columbia*, was launched by the United States of America on April 12, 1981.**

Space shuttles can withstand temperatures of 2,500°F (1,350°C).

Shuttles are the only spacecraft that can be re-launched and sent on further missions.

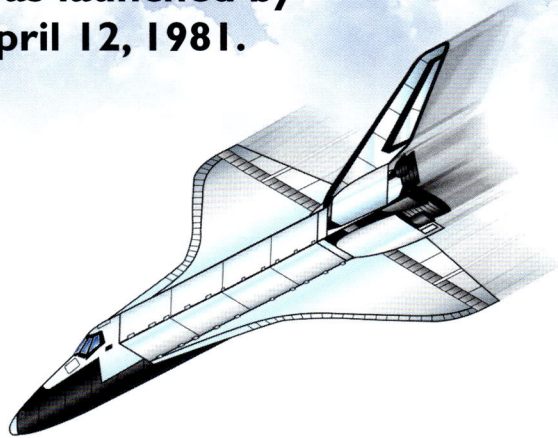

# H-II Rocket

**The Japanese National Space Development Agency hope to investigate the Sun, Moon, and Mars using a variation of the H-II rocket.**

The Japanese space program is entirely peaceful and commercial. It is against the law to use space technology for military purposes.

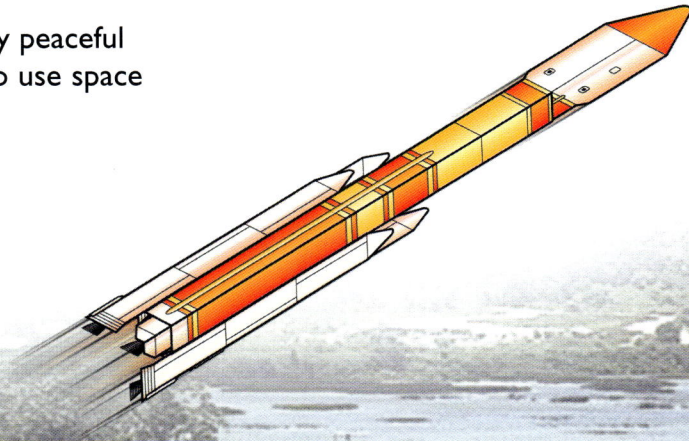

# Fokker Triplane Dr1

**The Fokker DR1 had three wings and was flown by the Germans in World War I. It could out-climb anything else in the sky. It could hide in the sun, then surprise other aircraft from above. Flown by a good pilot, it was very hard to beat.**

## Weaponry

The Fokker DR1 was armed with two Spandau machine guns. It had a top speed of 100 mph.

*The Fokker DRI triplane.*

## Death Trap

The Fokker DR1 was not popular with most German pilots. They never quite trusted it after some early DR1 aircraft actually lost their wings in mid-air.

*Fokker DR1's were not liked by German pilots.*

## The Red Baron

Only 300 Fokker DR1s were built, but they were made famous by Manfred von Richthofen, better known as the Red Baron. He shot down twenty of his eighty kills in a Fokker painted bright red.

*The famous Red Baron and his bright red Fokker DRI.*

## Twenty-four Days

One Fokker DR1 pilot was Lieutenant Voss. In 24 days of action during 1917, he shot down 21 aircraft. On September 23, 1917, he was shot down and killed by a British SE 5a biplane. He was nineteen years old.

# Sopwith Camel

**The Sopwith Camel was one of World War I's greatest fighter aircraft flown by British and U.S. pilots. It was fast and aerobatic. A good Camel pilot could shoot down anything else in the sky.**

## Size

The Camel was small, with a 28 ft wingspan. It was built from wood and cloth.

*Sopwith Camels were good fighter planes.*

*Sopwith Camels were difficult to fly.*

## Small, but Deadly

The Camel was armed with two Vickers machine guns that fired forward through the spin of the propeller. Pilots were trained to attack in a vertical dive, firing down on the enemy.

## High and Fast

The Sopwith Camel, could fly at over 100 mph, and up to 18,000 ft—high and fast for the time. The Camel could carry enough fuel for 2.5 hours of flight.

## Danger Machine

The Camel was a good fighter plane, but very difficult to fly. Nearly 400 Sopwith Camel pilots were killed in World War I, not by enemy fire, but by pilot errors.

*A Sopwith Camel.*

# Messerschmitt Bf 109

**In 1937, the Messerschmitt Bf 109 could fly at 388 mph, but only had a range of 425 miles. It was fast and deadly.**

## Weapons

The Messerschmitt Bf 109 was armed with two 13 mm machine guns on its wings, a 20 mm cannon in the center of the propeller, and two 20 mm cannons under the wings.

*Over 35,000 Bf 109's were built.*

## Super Fighter

The Messerschmitt Bf 109 shot down more enemy aircraft in World War II than any other German aircraft.

*The Messerschmitt Bf109—a heavily armed fighter.*

## Hard to Fly

Bf 109s were difficult to fly. They swung over to the left on takeoff and landing. Of all the Bf 109s, one in twenty crashed during takeoff or landing.

*The Messerschmitt Bf 109 was no match for Spitfires and Hurricanes.*

## Heavy Losses

Until the Battle of Britain in the summer and fall of 1940, the Bf 109 was unbeatable. However, fighting against Spitfires and Hurricanes, it began to lose. Over 600 were shot down.

## Long Service

It was in active service for over twenty years.

# P40 Warhawk

In World War II the Warhawk became known as the "Flying Tiger." It was used by the Americans for fighting against the Japanese in China and Burma. The Warhawk was also used a great deal in the Middle East by the British Royal Air Force (R.A.F.), who nicknamed it the Tomahawk, or Kittyhawk.

## Mass Produced

The Warhawk was the first American single-seater plane to be mass produced in the U.S.A., and was the only fighter available in quantity to the U.S.A.F. at the beginning of the war. By 1945, over 14,000 planes had been delivered.

*A P40 Warhawk, Dayton Airshow, Ohio, America, 1984.*

## Durable

Although the P40 Warhawk was not particularly good either technically or in performance, it was very sturdy and was able to endure many a fierce battle.

*A P40 Warhawk, Biggin Hill Airshow, Britain, 1999.*

# The Kingfisher

**The Kingfisher is famous for its ability to land on water. It can only do this because of the floats fitted to the body (fuselage) of the plane.**

### Savior of Men

The prototype Kingfisher OS2U first took to the air on March 1, 1938. The plane's early success in air-sea rescue led to it being known as "Kingfisher, Savior of Men."

*A Kingfisher landing on water.*

*Vaught OS2U Kingfisher.*

### Flying High

The Kingfisher was also used as an observation plane. Flying high above a sea or land target, the pilot would communicate by radio to his ship to tell the gunners how they should adjust the aim of the ship's guns.

# Focke-Wulf Fw 190

**The Focke-Wulf was one of the greatest German fighters of World War II. When it first appeared, it out-flew the best Allied aircraft, including the Spitfire.**

## Fighter Bomber

The Focke-Wulf was built for air-to-air combat and as a fighter-bomber. It carried four 20 mm cannons and two 13 mm machine guns.

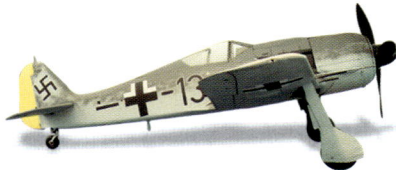

*The Focke-Wulf—a fighter bomber.*

## Head-on Attack

The Focke-Wulf would attack head on, where the bombers had the fewest guns. A pilot might have fifteen seconds to line up his target and fire. It took keen eyes and courage to make these assaults.

*Over 20,000 Focke-Wulf aircraft were built.*

## Gun Power

With all guns firing, a Focke-Wulf could let loose 70 rounds a second. The German air force estimated it could take around twenty rounds to bring down an American B-17 bomber.

*Focke-Wulfs carried out low-level bombing raids.*

## Flying Under Radar

In World War II, the Focke-Wulf made low-level bombing raids over the English Channel.

# Avro 683 Lancaster

**The Lancaster was built by the British and was without doubt the most successful heavy night bomber deployed over Europe during World War II.**

## The Mighty Bomber

The Lancaster bomber carried on average a 14,000 lb bomb load or a single 48,500 lb bomb and had ten machine guns. Powered by four Rolls-Royce Merlin XX Vee liquid-cooled engines, each driving a three-blade constant-speed and fully feathering propeller, its maximum speed was 287 mph and it had a flying range of 1,660 miles.

## Heavy, Slow, yet Reliable

With their 102 ft wingspan and powerful engines, they could climb up to 24,500 ft.

## The Admiral Prune

The most famous Lancaster was called Admiral Prune, and its squadron (617 Squadron) was commanded by Wing Commander Guy Gibson in 1942. Their most famous mission was the breaching of the Mohne and Eder Dams during World War II, using the "bouncing bomb."

*The Lancaster became the most used British bomber of World War II.*

# P-51 Mustang

**The P-51 Mustang was a fast and furious aircraft flown by the U.S. It was amazing because of its range; it could fly 1,500 miles.**

## Fastest Fighter

The P-51 Mustang could outrun a Spitfire at low level, and fly three times as far. It was even faster in production. It took only 102 days to design and build the first P-51.

*P-51 Mustangs acted as protection for bombers.*

*The Mustang carried six fifty-calibre machine guns. It could fly at 440 mph at 30,000 ft.*

## Long Service

The P-51 Mustang was an active fighter for over thirty years with air forces around the world.

## Little Friend

World War II bomber crews nicknamed the Mustang "Little Friend" because of its job as a bomber escort. In the early years of the war, it was the only fighter that could fly far enough to take bombers all the way to the German capital of Berlin. Bombers needed a lot of support; sometimes a third of the aircraft on a raid would be shot down.

# Hercules C130

**The Hercules C130 was designed by the British Royal Air Force. It has been used recently to deliver humanitarian relief to Haiti, Bosnia, Somalia, and Rwanda.**

## Workhorse

The Hercules C130 is the workhorse of the R.A.F. Used primarily for para-dropping troops and delivering equipment to hostile areas, it is capable of landing on rough, makeshift runways.

*The C130 can carry more than 42,000 lbs of cargo.*

## Other Roles

Basic and specialized versions of the aircraft are used to perform various roles around the globe including, air support, Arctic ice re-supply, aero-medical missions, aeriel spray missions, and fire-fighting duties for the U.S. Forest Service.

*Modified landing gear enables the C130 to land on rough and bumpy runways.*

## Versatility

Each role requires the basic model of the aircraft to be modified to enable it to carry out the required task. The Hercules is a versatile, reliable and effective addition to the R.A.F.'s operations.

*The C130 is one of the most versatile transport aircraft ever built.*

# MiG-21

The Russian MiG-21 was a very successful air-to-air fighter. The MiG-21 has been flown by more than thirty countries and has seen extensive combat action.

## Simple

The MiG-21 was simple, reliable and easy to maintain. Its delta-wing design gave it excellent handling abilities and a high top speed. The MiG-21 was difficult to fight, but its weakness was the short time it could stay in the air.

*The Russian MiG-2—one of the most successful fighters.*

## Lightly Armed

MiG-21s were armed with two heat-seeking missiles and one 23 mm cannon. Compared to many other fighter aircraft, they didn't have many weapons.

*MiG-21s are armed with heat-seeking missiles.*

## War Vet

MiG-21s fought against the U.S. in the Vietnam War. For the first time, aircraft fought miles apart with missiles, rather than at close range.

The MiG-21s were much faster than the American Phantom F-4s, but U.S. fighter-pilot training and weaponry were superior.

503

# Harrier "Jump Jet"

**The Harrier is the only fighter aircraft that can take off and land vertically (VTOL) anywhere—from a ship's deck to a small patch of grass.**

### Carbon Fiber Wings
The Harrier has wings built from single pieces of strong, light carbon fiber.

### Straight Up
The Harrier uses swiveling nozzles on its engine to give it vertical lift.

### Straight Down
Harriers are built to perform stunts and turns that no other aircraft can. One is known as vectoring, where the pilot suddenly shifts the direction of the harrier's nozzles, throwing the aircraft into a new attack position.

*The Harrier is a successful fighter aircraft.*

### Into Action
Harriers can be based close to the enemy, and can land near battlefields or ships of almost any size. They are built for air-to-air combat or ground attack missions. They can carry 25 mm guns, seven missiles and an array of extra fuel tanks.

*The Harrier Jump Jet—the only VTOL fighter.*

# Boeing 747

Boeing began developing the 747 after a request from the U.S.A.F. for a heavy cargo transporter. When the 747 was rejected as a military airplane Boeing decided to develop it as a commercial aircraft.

## Spacious

The plane made its maiden flight on February 9, 1969. Its enormous fuselage has room for rows of nine passengers and an upper deck.

*The 747 is probably the world's most famous carrier plane.*

*Over two billion people have flown in 747s.*

## Easy Operation

The 747 uses powered controls and advanced navigation systems so that only three flight crew are needed to operate the aircraft.

# MiG-25 Foxbat

**The Russian Foxbat was built as a high-level fighter. It can intercept cruise missiles and high-flying bombers. Its top speed of 2,115 mph makes it one of the fastest fighters in the world.**

## High Flier

The MiG-25 was built to fly high. At low levels it is slow and weak in a fight. It is the highest-flying jet, soaring to the edge of our atmosphere. It holds the world altitude record for a jet aircraft of 123,524 ft.

*The Foxbat is a high-performance fighter.*

*The MiG-25—known as the Foxbat.*

## Worldwide Fighter

The MiG-25 is used by air forces around the world. The Iraqi air force used MiGs in the Gulf War. The MiG-25 carries four air-to-air missiles with infrared and radar homing heads, but doesn't have guns.

## Hot Metal

As the MiG-25 blasts through the air at supersonic speed, its skin gets very hot. The MiG-25 has an outershell made of titanium that expands and contracts with the heat.

*The Foxbat has swept-back wings and two turbojet engines.*

# F-16 Falcon

The F-16 Fighting Falcon is a small, highly maneuverable, air-to-air combat aircraft flown by the U.S. It can attack at night and in all weather, even when the pilot can't see the target. Screens and electronic displays in the cockpit tell the pilot what is happening around him.

## Super Strong

The F-16 is so fast and turns so quickly that the aircraft can experience a gravitational force of 9g—about as much as a human can bear.

*The F-16 can deliver its weapons with incredible accuracy and defend itself against enemy aircraft.*

## Supersonic and Deadly

The F-16 can fly at more than Mach 2 (twice the speed of sound). Pilots stay in control with the help of fly-by-wire electronic equipment. The F-16 carries six air-to-air missiles and a 20 mm cannon with 500 rounds.

*The F-16 Fighting Falcon.*

## Pilot Training

F-16 pilots are trained to maneuver against attacks. It takes nerve and a lot of skill. During training, the forward cockpit is used by the student pilot, with the instructor pilot in the rear cockpit.

## Secret Signal

To make sure friendly forces don't shoot down their own fighters, the F-16 sends a secret radio signal to ground forces.

# B-1B Lancer

The B-1B Lancer was built by the U.S. as a long-range, multi-role, heavy bomber. It has the capability to fly intercontinental missions without needing to refuel.

## Adjustable Wings

B1-Bs have a swing-wing design and turbofan engines that provide a greater range and high speed at low levels. With the wing sweep at full forward position it all allows the B-1B a short takeoff roll and a fast base-escape profile from airfields under attack.

*The B-1B can fly at a height of over 30,000 ft.*

## Low and Fast

With four General Electric F-101-GE-102 turbofan engines with afterburner, the B-1B can reach speeds of over 900 mph (Mach 1.2 at sea level).

*The B-1B has a wing span of 137 ft when extended forward, and 79 ft when swept back.*

## Defense System

The B-1B's electronic jamming equipment, infrared countermeasures and radar location warning systems form a sophisticated, integrated defense system for the aircraft. With a crew of four (aircraft commander, pilot, offensive systems' operator and defense systems' officer), the B-1B is a force to be reckoned with.

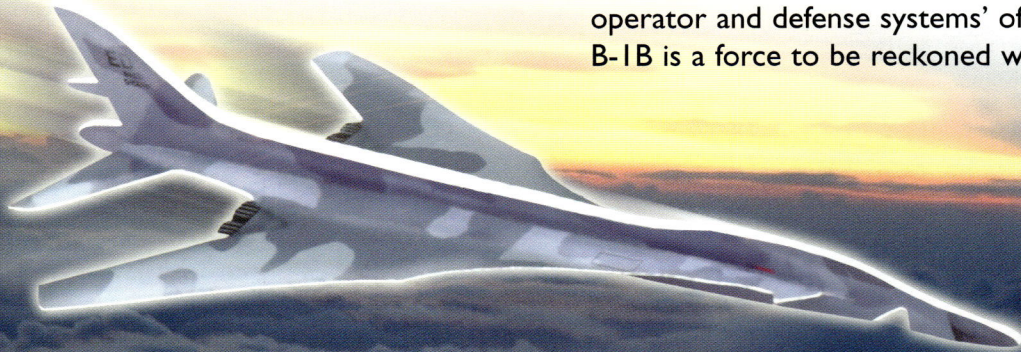

# YF-22 Raptor

**The YF-22 Raptor was commissioned by the U.S.A.F. in 1981. Production of the first 750 aircraft has begun and they should be ready to fly missions in 2004.**

### Stealth Technology

The air force wanted an Advanced Tactical Fighter (ATF) which would take advantage of new technologies in fighter design, including advanced flight control systems and stealth technology.

*The Raptor is an advanced tactical fighter.*

*The Raptor—one of the fastest planes around.*

### A Superior Fighter

The Raptor is a single-seater aircraft that can fly at heights of over 50,000 ft. Fitted with heat-seeking missiles and radar-guided air-to-air missiles, it is capable of flying at twice the speed of sound (Mach 2).

23

# F-104C Starfighter

**The F-104C Starfighter was intended to be a supersonic tactical strike fighter. The first F-104C took off on its maiden flight on July 24, 1958.**

### A Tactical Strikefighter

The F-104C was designed mainly for delivery of tactical nuclear weapons which it could carry on a centerline pylon attachment which had a 2,000 lb capacity. It could carry the Mark 28 and Mark 43 nuclear weapons. It could also carry bombs or rocket pods on underwing and fuselage points.

*A Starfighter in action.*

### Record Breaker

In 1959, the F-104C became the first aircraft taking off under its own power to fly at an altitude of over 100,000 ft.

# C-141 Starlifter

**The Lockheed C-141 Starlifter was built by the U.S. as a long-range, all-jet transport to extend the reach of the nation's military forces. It is capable of performing strategic and tactical airlift missions.**

## Versatility

The Starlifter is capable of providing low-altitude delivery of troops and equipment and high-altitude delivery of paratroops. It can also air drop equipment and supplies using the Container Delivery System (CDS).

*The C-141 Starlifter can airlift combat forces over long distances.*

## High Specifications

The Starlifter has a high-set wing sweep of 25 degrees and is used for high-speed cruising, with powerful flaps and slats provided for good low-speed field performance. The aircraft is powered by four under-wing TF33 turbofan engines and has integral wing fuel tanks.

*The C-141 Starlifter is able to refuel in flight.*

## Finest Hour

Possibly the Starlifter's finest hour was in the second half of 1990, during the Gulf War. America's entire fleet was responsible for transporting most of the equipment to Iraq, for operations Desert Shield and Desert Storm.

# Nimrod MRA4

**The Nimrod MRA4 is built in the United Kingdom. It is a maritime reconnaissance and attack aircraft, specializing in anti-submarine warfare, anti-surface unit warfare, and search and rescue.**

## Fighting Machine

Nimrods have a weapons bay with side-opening doors at the bottom of the fuselage, which can carry fuel tanks, torpedoes and sonobuoy floats equipped to defect and transmit under water noises. The wings have four weapons pylons for the carriage of Boeing AGM-84 Harpoon anti-ship missiles or AIM-9 Sidewinder air-to-air missiles.

*A Nimrod's cockpit is packed with hi-tech instruments and controls.*

*The Nimrod MRA4 specializes in anti-submarine warfare.*

## Power and Speed

The Nimrod has four BMW Rolls-Royce BR710 engines, which, together with its additional fuel capacity, can fly at Mach 0.77.

## Navigation

Navigational accuracy is provided by a Navigation and Flight Management System (NAV/FMS). It is highly advanced and, along with the Global Positioning Systems and a TCAS 2 Traffic Alert and Collision Avoidance System, it makes the Nimrod one of the safest aircraft, in our skies.

# Phantom F-4

**The Phantom was built by the U.S. to seek out and destroy enemy fighters and for ground attacks. It saw action in the Vietnam War and operation Desert Storm.**

## Foldaway Aircraft

The Phantom F-4 often flew from aircraft carriers. It had fold-up wings which took up less space than conventional wings, and hooks to snag cables on the deck of the carrier which helped it to stop.

*Phantom F-4s are all-weather fighter-bombers.*

## How to Win

To win a dogfight in a Phantom you had to use the aircraft's dive-and-climb speed and to be a good shot. The 20 mm cannon in the aircraft's nose had just 640 rounds—enough for 6.5 seconds of firing.

*A Phantom F-4 can refuel in mid-air.*

## Heavy but Fast

Phantoms were heavy but very powerful combat aircraft. They had a maximum speed of 1,500 mph. They could climb to 25,000 ft—nearly the height of Mount Everest—in just thirty seconds.

# A-10 Thunderbolt

The **A-10 Thunderbolt** was the first U.S. aircraft to provide day and night air support to ground forces. It saw action in the Gulf War and was vital during operation Desert Storm.

## Slight and Nippy

A-10s are simple twin-engine (two General Electric TF-4-100/A turbofan engines) jet aircraft. They have excellent maneuverability at low speeds. Capable of loitering near battle areas for extended periods of time, the A-10 can operate under 1,000 ft.

*The A-10 Thunderbolt can be used against tanks.*

## Munitions

The Thunderbolt's 30 mm GAU-8/A Gatling gun can fire 3,900 rounds of ammunition a minute. It can defeat and destroy many different ground targets, including tanks.

*The A-10 Thunderbolt can take off and land on short runways.*

## One Man at Speed

The Thunderbolt has just one crew member who is encased in a pressurized, titanium armor-plated cockpit and is capable of flying at speeds of up to 420 mph (Mach 0.56), at a heady height of 44,738 ft.

# SR-71 Blackbird

**The SR-71 was unofficially named the Blackbird. It was built by the U.S. as a long-range strategic reconnaissance and spy aircraft.**

## High Flier and Fast

The SR-71 is one of the most magnificent military aircraft ever built. Capable of flying at 85,000 ft, it has a range of 3,200 mph (without refueling). It has a maximum speed of 2,372 mph (Mach 3.3).

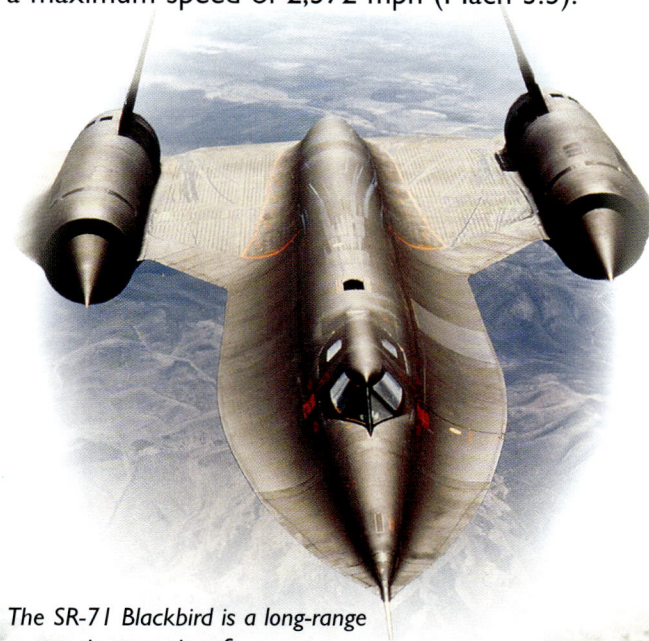

*The SR-71 Blackbird is the world's fastest jet plane.*

## Power and Reliability

The SR-71 is powered by two Pratt and Whitney J-58 jet engines. This aircraft has played an important military role in international conflicts for nearly thirty years.

## All Seeing Eye

The cameras on board the Blackbird are very powerful. They can photograph a golf ball from 80,000 ft, and they can survey 110,000 miles of Earth's surface in one hour.

*The SR-71 Blackbird is a long-range reconnaissance aircraft.*

# F-117A Nighthawk

The F-117A Nighthawk (Stealth Fighter) is designed to be invisible. Its angled shape and matt-black body absorbs and deflects radar. This fighter can attack and escape without being tracked. It was used by the U.S. in the Gulf War.

## Technology

Nighthawks use a variety of weapons, including an automated mission planning system.

*The unusual shape of the Nighthawk.*

*Nighthawks are designed to be invisible to the enemy.*

## Silent and Deadly

Early versions of the Nighthawk were very difficult to fly. However, today's Nighthawk is highly maneuveurable. The one thing it cannot do is fly slowly. Its landing speed is 171 mph, and it needs a parachute to stop.

## Invisible

Everything about the Nighthawk is built to be invisible. Its cockpit glass is coated in gold to reflect enemy radar. Its exhausts are wide and flat so it leaves a small heat trail. Even its bomb doors are jagged to avoid radar detection.

## Elevons

Ordinary aircraft have both rudders and ailerons that control side-to-side and up-and-down movement. The Nighthawk has elevons, a control device that combines the functions of the rudders and ailerons. Many of the aircraft's parts are made of aluminum and titanium. The outer surface of the aircraft is coated with a radar-absorbent material.

# F/A-18 Hornet

The F/A-18 Hornet is an all-weather fighter and attack aircraft. A single-seater aircraft, it is designed for traditional strike applications such as interdiction and close-air support.

## Strike-fighter

The F/A-18 Hornet was used in operation Desert Storm during the Gulf War to shoot down enemy fighters and bomb enemy targets.

*The Hornet is designed for interdiction—destruction by firepower.*

## Versatile

The latest Hornet models are capable of air superiority, fighter escort, reconnaissance, aerial refueling, close-air support, air defense suppression and day/night precision strikes.

*Hornets can refuel in the air.*

# Design and Fly Paper Airplanes

**Make some amazing flying models from the templates provided on the CD in your pack.**

## Running the CD

If you are using a PC, the program should run automatically. If not, double click on the "my computer" icon on the desktop, and then on the "CD drive" icon. Then double click on the title "art-pc.exe."

If you are using a Macintosh© double click on the "CD" icon on the desktop, and then double click on the title "art-mac."

## Minimum System Requirements

• Screen resolution 800 x 600
• CD-ROM color depth 24-bit (true color)

PC users—Intel Pentium© 166 processor running Windows TM 95/98 or NT version 4.0 or later, 64 MB of installed RAM and a color monitor.

Macintosh© users—Power PC running System 8.1 or later, 64 MB of installed RAM and a color monitor.

## Printing the Templates

Before you print any of the images from the CD-ROM, check the printer settings under the "File" menu and make sure that you've selected "quality paper." Aim to use thin but high-quality paper for the best results! Check that you have selected the "Portrait" setting under the "Page Setup" menu.

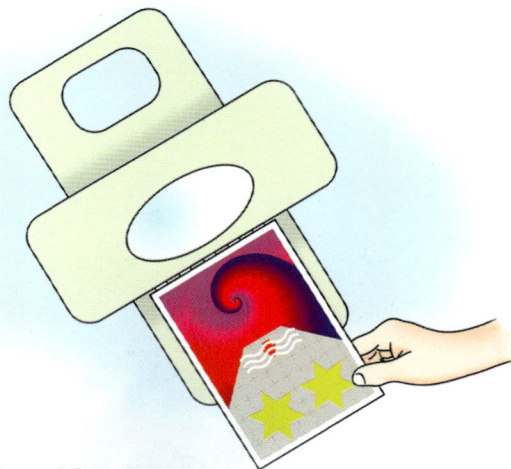

## Loading Up...

Once your CD has loaded, a welcome page will appear. Click on "Enter" to go onto the next page. When you've done this, a screen will appear offering you three options. Click on "Create" and the studio will appear. This is where you put the templates together.

## The Drawers

You will find five drawers on the left-hand side of the screen. They open and close with one click of the mouse. You'll build up your plane by taking parts out of each.

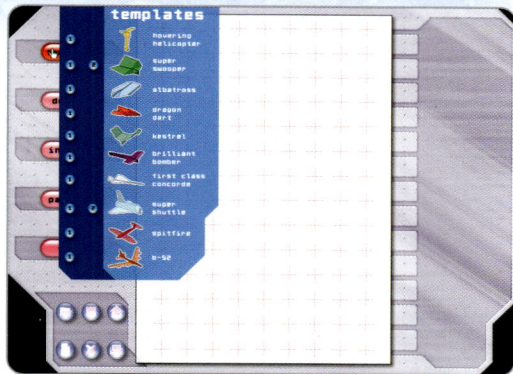

## The Pasteboard

The pasteboard is the gray panel down the right-hand side of the screen. The parts you've taken out of each drawer appear here. To move the parts onto the main screen, close the drawer, click on the part and drag it over. You can put a maximum of 24 images onto the board. Images will overlap on the pasteboard, but click on the one you want and it will pop up.

## The Blank Page

The blank page is the white rectangle with red crosses that appears in the centre of the page when the studio first loads. It is the only part of the screen that will print out. Once you have chosen a template, it will fill the page and you can start adding more parts to your plane.

## What's What?

The icons at the bottom left-hand corner of the screen are short cuts that leave you more time to be creative! Here's what they all mean:

Home—click on the "home" icon to return to the main menu. (You also need to do this to 'escape' the program.)

Cross—click on the "cross" icon to delete any parts you've chosen from the drawers, such as shapes and accessories. Highlight, then click on the "X."

Page—click on the "page" icon to delete a whole page. When you finish one project and start the next, you also have to delete the images left on the pasteboard.

Print—click on the "printer" icon to print your work at any stage. If your project is slow in printing, quit the program to speed it up.

Save—you can save your work at any time by clicking on the "disk" icon. Give your file a name when you save it, and choose somewhere suitable to put it, such as your desktop.
To resave it, click on the icon again. You will have to re-type your file name to save it again. An alert box will then pop up asking you whether you wish to replace the original. Click "Yes" if you have a PC, and "Replace" if you have a Macintosh©.

Open—open a file by clicking on the "open file" icon. Create a folder in which to save it.

# The Toolkit

The five drawers contain all you need to create a fantastic plane, which you will then cut and fold to make it three-dimensional. When starting out, it's easiest to work through these drawers roughly in the order shown below. Remember, you must close one drawer before you can open another.

## Template

1. Open the "Templates" drawer to see pictures of all the models. The numbers to the left of each picture refer to the number of templates required to make up each model.

2. Choose a design that you like, and click on the numbered buttons to fill the screen with that template. Close the drawer.

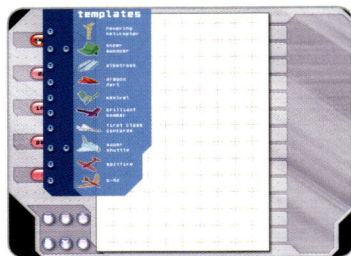

## Details

The shading on the template represents the parts of the plane that are visible when the model is folded up.

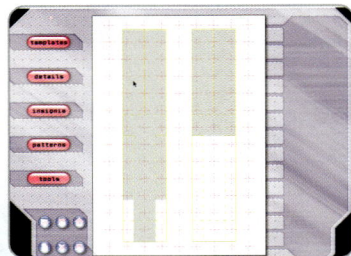

1. Open the "Details" drawer and a grid will appear, displaying all the designs you can choose from. On the top of the grid you will be able to see which page you are on, and how many designs there are in total. To view the next page, click on the right-hand arrow. To view the previous page, click on the left-hand arrow.

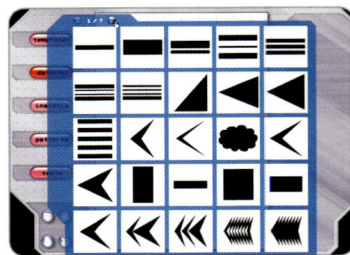

2. Click on the items that you need and they will appear on the pasteboard. The grid overlay is designed to help you place details onto the gray areas as precisely as possible.

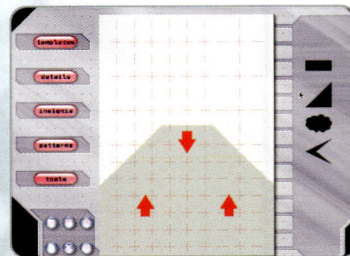

34

**3.** Simply drag the item from the pasteboard towards the gray area. The centre of the item will "snap" to the lines present on the grid. You can, of course, place items anywhere outside the gray area and the grid system will still work. Just remember that these details may be hidden by your folds later. Have fun experimenting!

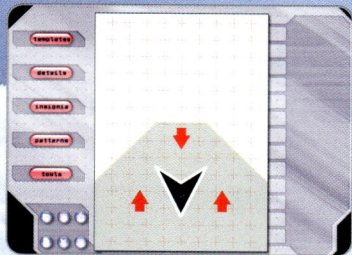

## Insignia

The "Insignia" drawer contains loads of cool signs and symbols that you can place anywhere on the template to personalize your plane.

**1.** To select, simply open the drawer, click on the insiginia you want, and it will appear on the pasteboard.

**2.** Close the drawer, and then experiment with where you want to place the image by dragging it over the template, then releasing.

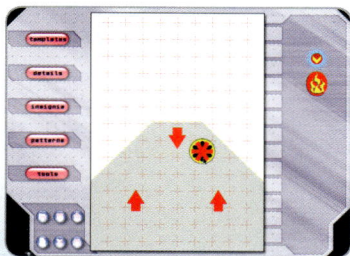

## Patterns

Does the template look a bit boring? Well, don't worry, You can change the entire background color!

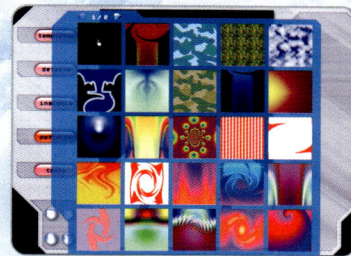

**1.** Simply click on any gray part of the template and open the "Patterns" drawer. You'll see lots of different patterns on a grid. If you like camouflage, or any other pattern, simply click on it. If you want to make it a plain colour, you need to make the background black first, so click on the black square.

**2.** When you close the drawer, you'll find that the template has filled with your chosen color! Remember, if you don't like the pattern you've chosen, simply re-open the "Patterns" drawer, and click on another box in the grid.

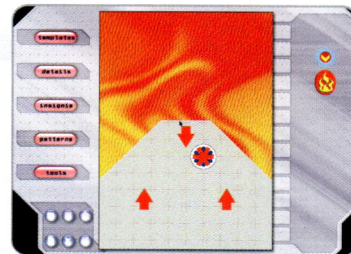

# Tools

This drawer contains two main functions. When you open it, you'll see the buttons that change your images and the "color mixer." Here's what they can do:

## Images

You can alter the size and position of images chosen from the "Details" and "Insignia" drawers.

### 1. Making images larger and smaller

Highlight the image and click on either the + or the − button until it is the required size.
You can click on the opposite button if the image gets too large or too small.

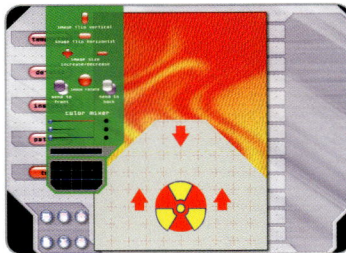

### 2. Flipping images

Highlight the image and click on the vertical button to turn it upside down, or the horizontal button to switch it to either side.

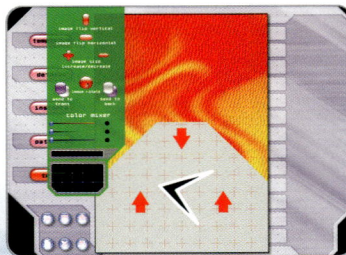

### 3. Layering images

If you drag an image from the pasteboard onto the template and then drop another over it, the first will always be behind the other.
If you want to reverse the image order, simply click on the "send to front" icon and it will bring the first image to the front. To change it back, simply click the "send to back" icon.

### 4. Rotate images

When you drag your item from the pasteboard, it may not be at the correct angle. This tool allows you to rotate items to fit within the dotted gray areas of the template. Drag the item onto the template itself, click to highlight, and then click on the red "image rotate" icon. This will turn your item 15 degrees with each click of the mouse.

## The Color Palette

This great tool allows you to change the color of your background and plane details with no fuss.

## Color Mixer
### 1. Light and Dark

Open the "Tools" drawer and you'll see three horizontal lines with blue circles to the left-hand side of each. Click on a circle and, when a "hand" icon appears, drag it slowly to the right. You'll see the colour getting lighter in the circle on the right-hand side of the line.

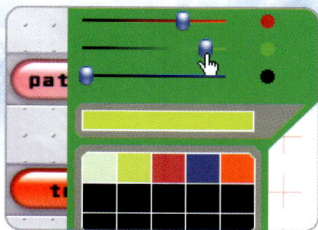

## 2. Fixing the Color

When you're happy with the color, release the mouse and double-click on the rectangle below. Magic! The color is stored in the grid-style palette. Keep going until you have all the colors you need.

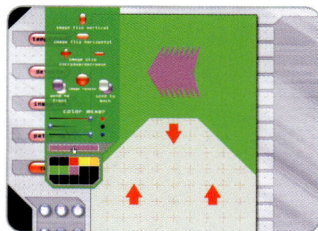

## Using the Colors

You can change the color of anything that is plain black. This includes the background and any black images selected from the "Details" drawer.

### HINT

You can mix any color of your choice by combining two or three color bars. You will need to determine which colors must be combined to make the color you want. Yellow is made from red and green, so drag one bar to red, another to green and yellow will appear in the rectangle. Double click on the rectangle to save the new color in the palette. You can put 15 colors in the palette.

## 1. Background

(A) To change the background to one plain color, go to the "Patterns" drawer and select the black square from the grid. Close this drawer, click on the background to highlight it, and then open the "Tools" drawer.

(B) Selecting any color you've mixed in your palette will change the background to the shade of your choice. Close the drawer to get the full effect! You can only change the color of the solid black background, not the patterned ones.

## 2. Details

(A) To change any black images from the "Details" drawer, simply highlight the part you want to change.

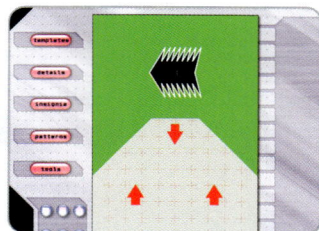

(B) Open the "Tools" drawer and click on a colour of your choice from the palette. Close the drawer. Of course, you can change the color if you are unsure simply by highlighting the image and repeating this process.

## 3. Printing

Once you are happy with the overall look of your template, save again and click on the "printer" icon in the bottom left-hand corner of the studio.

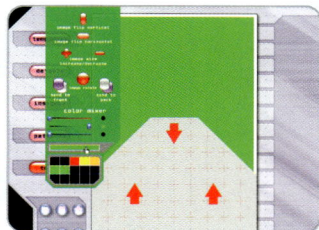

# Hovering Helicopter

## You will need:
- **a completed Hovering Helicopter template**
- **scissors**

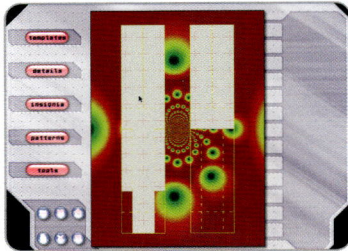

**1.** Cut along all the solid lines marked on your template.

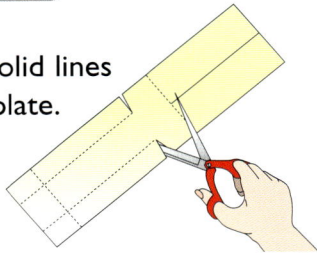

**2.** Fold flap A forward, and flap B to the back.

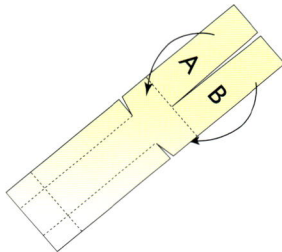

**3.** Fold both flaps C and D forward along the dotted lines. (Fold the entire length of the template, including part E.)

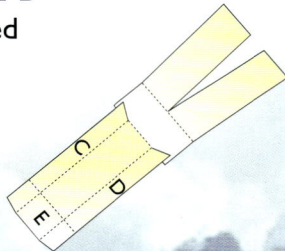

**4.** Fold along the horizontal line E, and then fold the flap upward to add some weight to the helicopter.

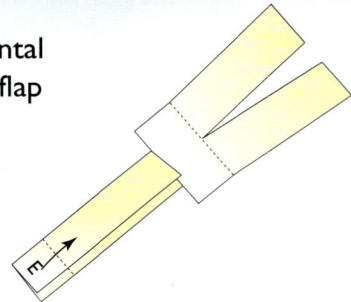

**5.** Make sure the blades are folded horizontally to each other, and then drop the helicopter from a height (such as from the top of the stairs). It will stay in the air for a long time, spiraling quickly as it comes down.

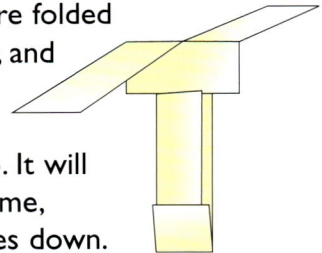

# Super Swooper

**Flying Tip!**
• Hold the Super Swooper just under the nose and throw it overhand with a slight upward push.

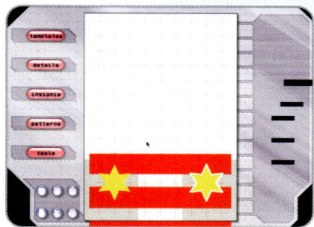

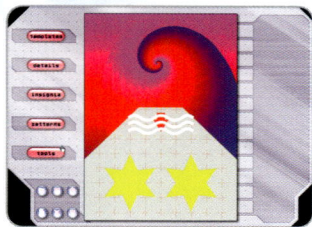

## You will need:
• completed Super Swooper plane templates

**1.** Print Template 1, then put the paper back in the printer and print Template 2 on the reverse. With Template 1 face down, fold the top left-hand corner down to touch the right-hand side to make a triangle.

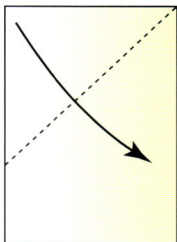

**2.** Fold the top point of the model down to reach the bottom-left hand side of the triangle. You should now have a house-shaped model, made from a rectangle with a triangle on the top.

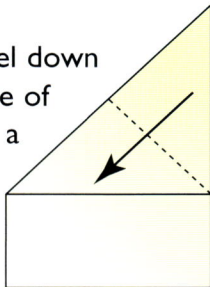

**3.** Fold the top point of the triangle down to reach one-third of the way up the rectangle below it.

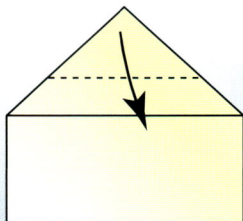

**4.** Fold the overlapping tip of the triangle under the flap beneath it.

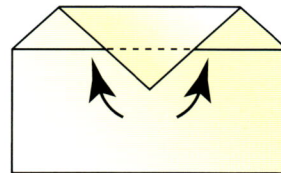

**5.** Fold the model in half from left to right.

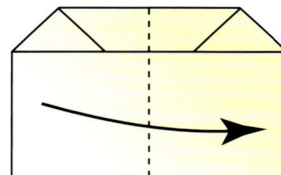

**6.** Fold down each side of the model to form the wings.

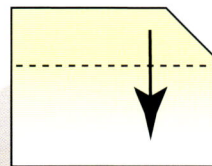

# Albatross

## You will need:
- **a completed Albatross template**

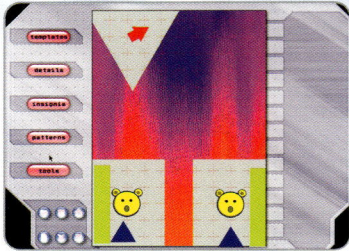

**1.** Place the template colored side down. Fold the template in half vertically from left to right and then unfold it leaving a crease.

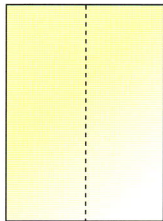

**2.** Fold the bottom left-hand corner about two-thirds across, as shown.

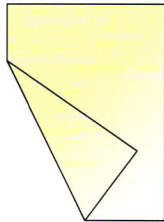

**3.** Repeat Step 2 with the right-hand corner, as shown, leaving a slight triangle to overlap the model.

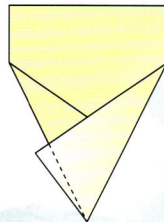

**4.** Turn the plane over, and fold the nose upwards to lie along the dotted line, as shown.

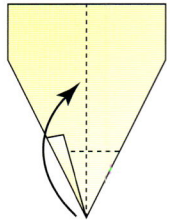

**5.** Fold and unfold along the centre line, and then make two vertical creases about 1 in. away from each side of it, as shown.

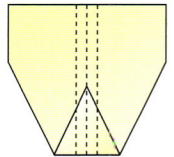

**6.** Make folds at the end of each wing, as shown. Make sure that they fold downward or the plane will fly upside down!

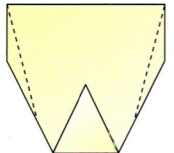

# Dragon Dart

## You will need:
• a completed Dragon Dart template

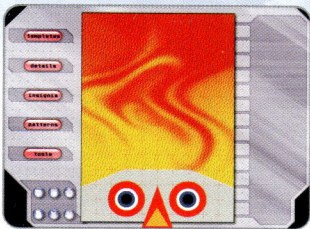

**1.** Place the template colored side down. Fold and unfold the template vertically, from left to right.

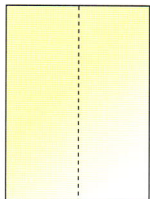

**2.** Fold the top left- and right-hand corners to the central crease.

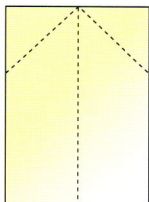

**3.** Fold the top left and right edges to lie along the central crease, along the dotted lines shown.

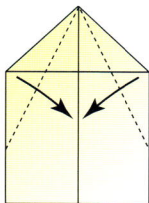

**4.** Fold the top point of the model downward to lie along the dotted line, as shown.

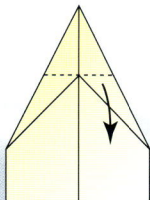

**5.** Fold the top right and left corners along the diagonal dotted lines, as shown, to meet the central crease.

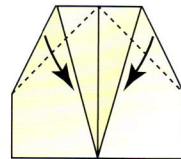

**6.** Fold the downward-facing triangular flap upward so that its tip touches the top of the model. It is very important that the tip meets the top point as neatly as possible.

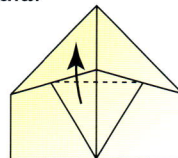

**7.** Fold the model in half. The side view should look like this.

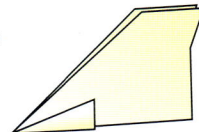

**8.** To make the wings, fold along the dotted lines shown in the diagram.

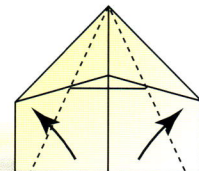

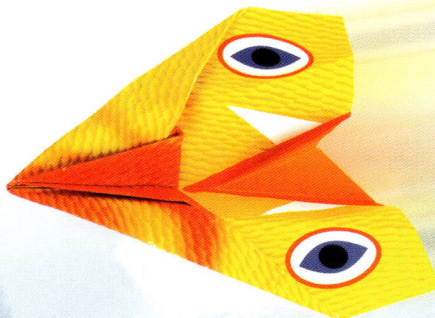

41

# Kestrel

## You will need:
- **a completed Kestrel template**

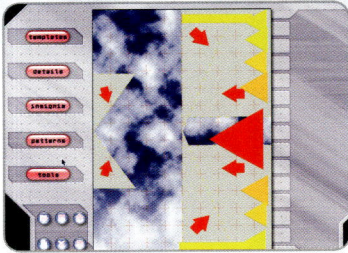

**1.** Place your template colored side down, triangles to the left. Fold the opposite edges together in turn, press flat and open up.

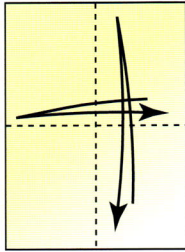

**2.** Fold the left-hand corners over, as shown. Then fold the left-hand point over to meet the middle of the opposite side.

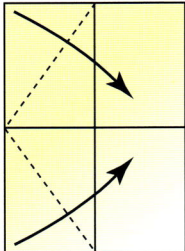

**3.** Again, fold the left-hand corners over.

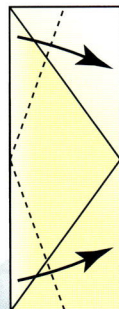

**4.** Fold the sloping edges under, as shown.

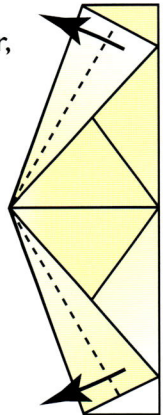

**5.** Fold the right-hand triangle over to the left.

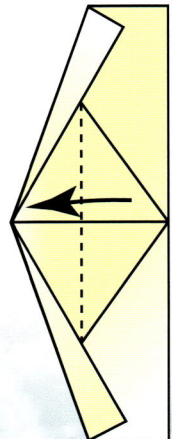

42

**6.** Fold the bottom edge behind to meet the top edge.

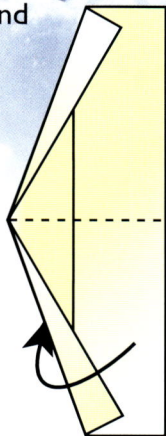

**7.** Fold the front flap forward and the back flap behind, making the wings.

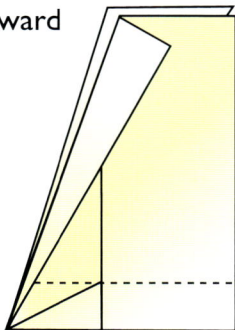

**8.** Fold the front wing up. Repeat behind.

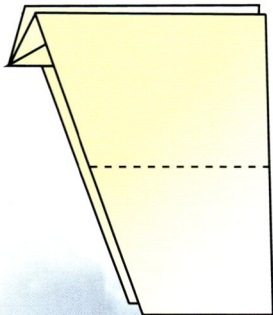

**9.** Fold a little of the front wing's top edge behind. Repeat with the back wing.

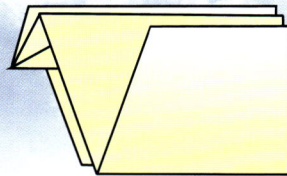

**10.** Open out the wings, as shown. This completes the Kestrel.

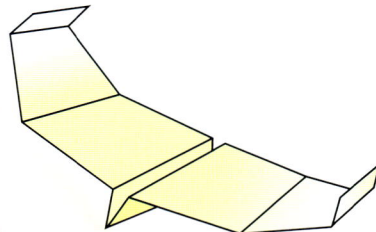

**Flying Tip!**
•Throw high up, fairly gently, and watch the Kestrel float gracefully downward.

# Brilliant Bomber

**You will need:**
- a completed **Brilliant Bomber template**
- a pair of scissors
- a paperclip

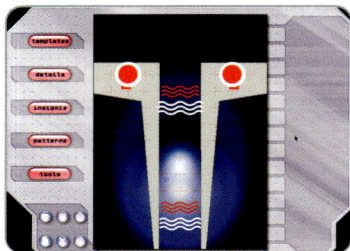

**1.** Make three folds across the template, as shown, using the dotted lines as a guide.

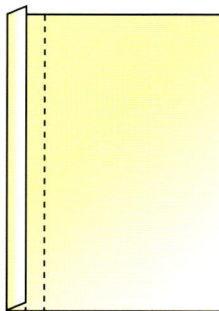

**2.** Fold the template in half from top to bottom, and cut away a section as indicated by the cutting marks on the template.

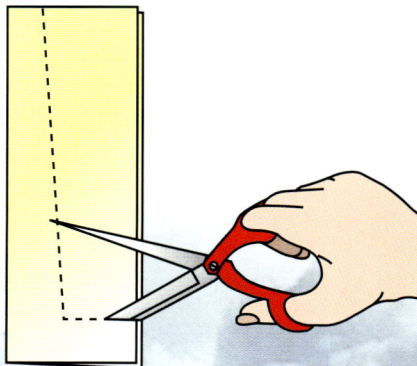

**3.** Fold down the wings, in the position indicated by the dotted lines on the template. Add a paperclip to the nose, and it's ready to fly!

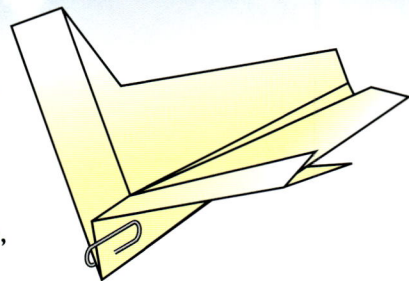

**Flying Tip!**
- Change the depth, angle, and size of the cut in Step 2 to increase the number of tricks your bomber is able to perform.

44

# 1st-Class Concorde

**You will need:**
- a completed Concorde template
- a piece of card
- glue
- scissors
- sticky putty

**Flying Tip!**
- Hold your Concorde between your thumb and forefinger, in front of the wings. Hold it above your shoulder and throw hard, with the front slightly raised.

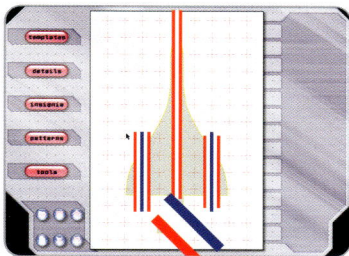

**1.** Stick your template onto thin card, and cut it out.

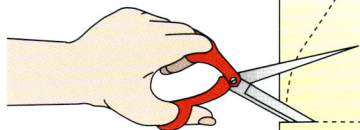

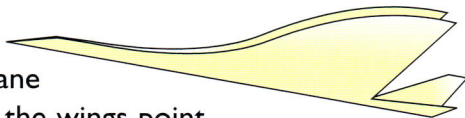

**2.** Fold the plane in half so that the wings point upward. Make sure that the wings are the same size. Planes with uneven wings may crash!

**3.** Open out the wings and angle them, as shown.

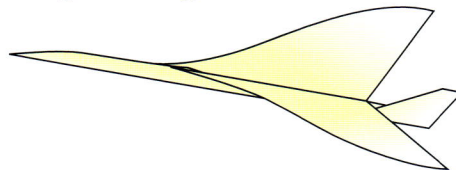

**4.** Stick a piece of sticky putty under the nose.

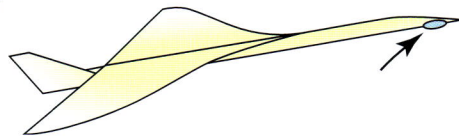

45

# Super Shuttle

**Flying Tip!**
• To launch your Super Shuttle, gently grip it at the back, hold it in front of your shoulder, and throw it forward with the front raised.

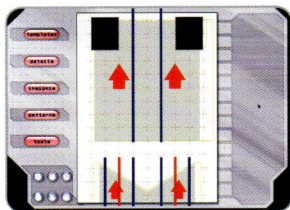

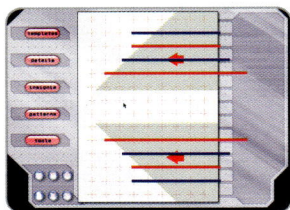

## You will need:
- a sheet of paper
- two completed Super Shuttle templates
- scissors
- tape
- two paperclips

**1.** Roll the piece of paper to make a cylinder with a diameter of 2 in. Use tape to hold it together.

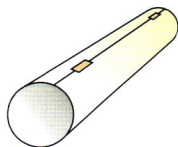

**2.** Fold Template 1 in half from left to right along the dotted lines indicated on the template. Then fold the left- and right-hand corners to the center fold.

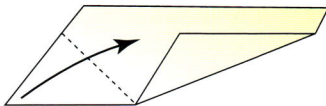

**3.** Tape the assembled cylinder onto Template 1. This forms the body and wings of the space shuttle.

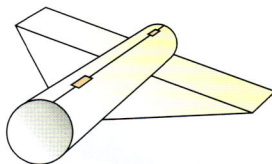

**4.** Cut the rectangle from Template 2, fold it in half along the dotted line, then fold up the tabs at both ends.

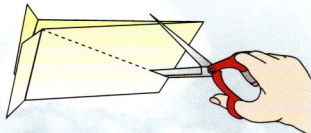

**5.** Cut a fin shape along the cutting lines of the template and stick it to the back of the cylinder.

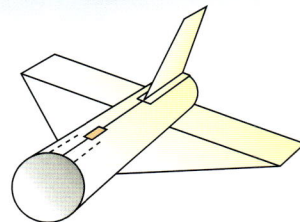

**6.** Cut slots measuring $1\frac{1}{2}$ in. along the nose-end of the cylinder. Fold down the resulting flap to form the cockpit.

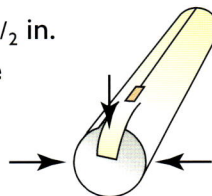

**7.** Finally, attach two paperclips to the nose of the Super Shuttle.

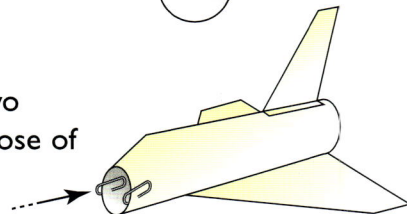

# Famous Replicas

The next two planes can be made simply by printing the templates onto thin card, cutting around the shapes, and slotting them together.

## You will need:
• a completed Spitfire template
• scissors

*A Supermarine Spitfire.*

## Spitfire

The Spitfire was the Allies' most important airplane in World War II. Its main opponent was the German Messerschmitt Bf 109. The Spitfire's markings made it a very distinctive airplane.

**1.** Design your templates on the page using the images, patterns and text from the CD. Print them out onto thin card.

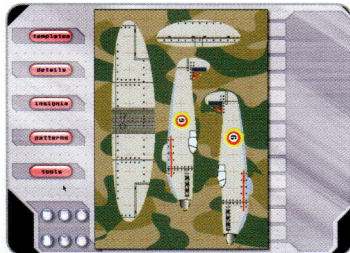

**2.** Make small cuts along the dotted lines shown on the templates.

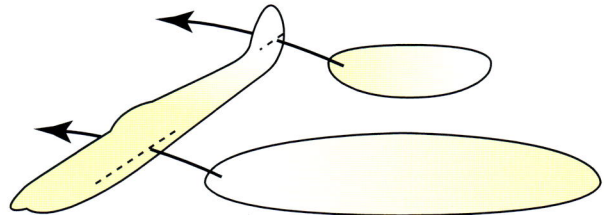

**3.** Slot the templates together.

# B-52 Stratofortress

## You will need:
- **a completed B-52 template**
- **scissors**

*A Boeing B-52 Stratofortress.*

## B-52 Stratofortress

The B-52 Stratofortress is probably the most important plane in the U.S. Air Force. It can carry a wide range of weapons, can refuel in mid-air, has a combat range of more than 8,700 miles, and can fly at subsonic speeds at altitudes of more than 50,000 ft. It made its first flight in 1954, and its technology has been updated ever since.

**1.** Design your templates on the page using the images, patterns and text from the CD. Print them out onto thin card.

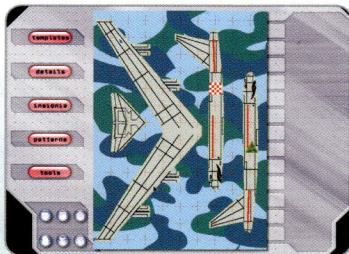

**2.** Make small cuts along the dotted lines shown on the templates.

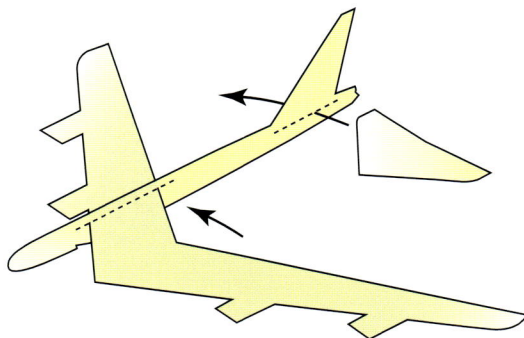

**3.** Slot the templates together.